Ten Poems ab

Candlestick Press

Published by:

Candlestick Press,

Diversity House, 72 Nottingham Road, Arnold, Nottingham UK NG5 6LF
www.candlestickpress.co.uk

Printed by Ratcliff & Roper Print Group, Nottinghamshire, UK

Selection and Introduction © Mahendra Solanki, 2017

Cover illustration © Sarah Kirby, 2017 www.sarahkirby.co.uk

Candlestick Press monogram © Barbara Shaw, 2008

© Candlestick Press, 2017
Reprinted 2018

Donation to Shelter www.shelter.org.uk

ISBN 978 1 907598 44 9

Acknowledgements:

The poems in this pamphlet are reprinted from the following books, all by
permission of the publishers listed unless stated otherwise. Every effort has
been made to trace the copyright holders of the poems published in this book.
The editor and publisher apologise if any material has been included without
permission or without the appropriate acknowledgement, and would be glad
to be told of anyone who has not been consulted. Thanks are due to all the
copyright holders cited below for their kind permission:

CP Cavafy, *The Selected Poems of Cavafy by CP Cavafy*, edited and translated
by Avi Sharon (Penguin Classics 2008). Translation and editorial matter
copyright © Avi Sharon, 2008.

Imtiaz Dharker, *I Speak for the Devil* (Bloodaxe Books, 2001)
www.bloodaxebooks.com

Tony Harrison, *Selected and Collected Poems* (Penguin, 2007),
by permission of Faber & Faber.

Linda Hogan, *Dark. Sweet.* (Coffee House Press, 2014). Copyright © 2014 by
Linda Hogan. By permission of Coffee House Press.

Phillip Larkin, *Collected Poems* (Faber; FSG, 2003) Copyright © 1988, 2003
by the Estate of Philip Larkin.

Grace Nichols, *I Have Crossed an Ocean: Selected Poems* (Bloodaxe Books,
2010) by permission of Curtis Brown UK.

Mahendra Solanki, poem as yet unpublished, by kind permission of the author.

Wislawa Szymborska, *MAPS: Collected and Lost Poems of Wislawa
Szymborska*, trans. from the Polish by Stanislaw Baranczak and Clare
Cavanagh, English Translation copyright (c) 2015 Houghton Mifflin Harcourt
Publishing Company. By permission of the publisher, all rights reserved.

Where poets are no longer living, their dates are given.

Introduction

According to the philosopher Gaston Bachelard, a house is our first universe as children. It is "the shelter of our imagination itself, a nest for dreaming" and probably why our daydreaming carries us back to it, to its "maternal paradise".

Homes house memories, however temporary. I remember staying in a cottage on an isolated farm in Scotland and recalling Ted Hughes' opening lines from his poem, 'Wind', to locate my feelings: "This house has been far out at sea all night, / The woods crashing through darkness, the booming hills, / Winds stampeding the fields under the window / floundering black astride and blinding wet".

We all have reasons to be where we are, or want to be. I write this introduction in an old cottage which has been my home for almost a dozen years, surrounded by packed boxes as I plan to move to another, probably my final home. We sometimes grow out of the homes we find ourselves in and perhaps seek light or escape in new dwellings, hoping this time round, we can be ourselves. As Maya Angelou says, "I long, as does every human being, to be at home wherever I find myself."

Salman Rushdie took Dorothy (in the Wizard of Oz) to task for saying, "There is no place like home" and resists the notion of 'home is where the heart is', preferring to think of home as somewhere you find yourself, or even homes that are made for you. The reclusive Emily Dickinson typically said it more succinctly, "Where thou art - that - is Home."

In selecting these poems, I was guided by a range of thoughts and emotions and in trying to find a balance between themes and voices, I was reminded of Joan Didion's acute observation, "The impulse for much writing is homesickness. You are trying to get back home, and in your writing you are invoking that home, so you are assuaging the homesickness."

Mahendra Solanki

The Lake Isle of Innisfree

I will arise and go now, and go to Innisfree,
And a small cabin build there, of clay and wattles made:
Nine bean-rows will I have there, a hive for the honey-bee,
And live alone in the bee-loud glade.

And I shall have some peace there, for peace comes dropping slow,
Dropping from the veils of the morning to where the cricket sings;
There midnight's all a glimmer, and noon a purple glow,
And evening full of the linnet's wings.

I will arise and go now, for always night and day
I hear lake water lapping with low sounds by the shore;
While I stand on the roadway, or on the pavements grey,
I hear it in the deep heart's core.

WB Yeats (1865 – 1939)

This room

This room is breaking out
of itself, cracking through
its own walls
in search of space, light,
empty air.

The bed is lifting out of
its nightmares.
From dark corners, chairs
are rising up to crash through clouds.

This is the time and place
to be alive:
when the daily furniture of our lives
stirs, when the improbable arrives.
Pots and pans bang together
in celebration, clang
past the crowd of garlic, onions, spices,
fly by the ceiling fan.
No one is looking for the door.

In all this excitement
I'm wondering where
I've left my feet, and why

my hands are outside, clapping.

Imtiaz Dharker

Home is so Sad

Home is so sad. It stays as it was left,
Shaped to the comfort of the last to go
As if to win them back. Instead, bereft
Of anyone to please, it withers so,
Having no heart to put aside the theft

And turn again to what it started as,
A joyous shot at how things ought to be,
Long fallen wide. You can see how it was:
Look at the pictures and the cutlery.
The music in the piano stool. That vase.

Philip Larkin (1922 – 1985)

Long Distance

i

Your bed's got two wrong sides. Your life's all grouse.
I let your phone-call take its dismal course:

Ah can't stand it no more, this empty house!

Carrots choke us wi'out your mam's white sauce!

Them sweets you brought me, you can have 'em back.
Ah'm diabetic now. Got all the facts.
(The diabetes comes hard on the track
of two coronaries and cataracts.)

Ah've allus liked things sweet! But now ah push
food down mi throat! Ah'd sooner do wi'out.
And t'only reason now for beer 's to flush
(so t'dietician said) mi kidneys out.

When I come round, they'll be laid out, the sweets,
Lifesavers, my father's New World treats,
still in the big brown bag, and only bought
rushing through JFK as a last thought.

ii

Though my mother was already two years dead
Dad kept her slippers warming by the gas,
put hot water bottles her side of the bed
and still went to renew her transport pass.

You couldn't just drop in. You had to phone.
He'd put you off an hour to give him time
to clear away her things and look alone
as though his still raw love were such a crime.

He couldn't risk my blight of disbelief
though sure that very soon he'd hear her key
scrape in the rusted lock and end his grief.
He *knew* she'd just popped out to get the tea.

I believe life ends with death, and that is all.
You haven't both gone shopping; just the same,
in my new black leather phone book there's your name
and the disconnected number I still call.

Tony Harrison

The Afternoon Sun

This room, how well I know it.
Now they're renting it, and the one next to it,
as offices. The whole house has become
an office building for agents, businessmen, companies.

This room, how familiar it is.

The couch was here, near the door,
a Turkish carpet in front of it.
Close by, the shelf with two yellow vases.
On the right—no, opposite—a wardrobe with a mirror.
In the middle the table where he wrote,
and the three big wicker chairs.
Beside the window the bed
where we made love so many times.

They must still be around somewhere, those old things.

Beside the window the bed;
the afternoon sun used to touch half of it.

. . . One afternoon at four o'clock we separated
for a week only. . . And then—
that week became forever.

CP Cavafy (1863 – 1933)
Translated by Edmund Keeley and Philip Sherrard

The Self-Unseeing

Here is the ancient floor,
Footworn and hollowed and thin,
Here was the former door
Where the dead feet walked in.

She sat here in her chair,
Smiling into the fire;
He who played stood there,
Bowing it higher and higher.

Childlike, I danced in a dream;
Blessings emblazoned that day;
Everything glowed with a gleam;
Yet we were looking away!

Thomas Hardy (1840 – 1928)

Crossings

There is a place at the center of earth
where one ocean dissolves inside the other
in a black and holy love;
It's why the whales of one sea
know songs of the other,
why one thing becomes something else
and sand falls down the hourglass
into another time.

Once I saw a fetal whale
on a block of shining ice.
Not yet whale, it still wore the shadow
of a human face, and fingers that had grown before the taking
back and turning to fin.
It was a child from the curving world
of water turned square,
cold, small.

Sometimes the longing in me
comes from when I remember
the terrain of crossed beginnings
when whales lived on land
and we stepped out of water
to enter our lives in air.

Sometimes it's from the spilled cup of a child
who passed through all the elements
into the human fold,
but when I turned him over
I saw that he did not want to live
in air. He'd barely lost
the trace of gill slits
and already he was a member of the clan of crossings.
Like tides of water,
he wanted to turn back.

I spoke across elements
as he was leaving
and told him, Go.
I was like the wild horses
that night when fog lifted.
They were swimming across the river.
Dark was that water,
darker still the horses,
and then they were gone.

Linda Hogan

To My Coral Bones

Deep
I Cariwoma
have always
carried deep
these islands,
this piece
of Atlantic coastland
inside me.
Sky-deep
Sea-deep
As star is to stone
As tide is to shore
Is just so I hold
these islands
to my coral bones.
And long before
hurricane strike,
some little butterfly,
some little blue messenger
of the soul will ride
the wind to bring
first news to my door.

Grace Nichols

Home

I am at home here, among
the priest's paraphernalia:
the incense, the tulsi leaves,
carefully measured amounts
of rice, flour, cotton, saffron
threads; items from a prescribed
list, long rehearsed with newly-
found aunts and long-lost uncles.

It's what brings us back to earth,
another ritual, at home.

Mahendra Solanki

Going Home

He came home. Said nothing.
It was clear, though, that something had gone wrong.
He lay down fully dressed.
Pulled the blanket over his head.
Tucked up his knees.
He's nearly forty, but not at the moment.
He exists just as he did inside his mother's womb,
clad in seven walls of skin, in sheltered darkness.
Tomorrow he'll give a lecture
on homeostasis in megagalactic cosmonautics.
For now, though, he has curled up and gone to sleep.

Wislawa Szymborska (1923 – 2012)